# How t

# NO
# TO YOUR
# PHONE

WRITTEN BY
**BRAD MARSHALL**
*THE UNPLUGGED PSYCHOLOGIST*
**AND LINDSAY HASSOCK**

ILLUSTRATED BY
**LAURIANE BOHÉMIER**

## MAGIC CAT PUBLISHING

*TO ALL THE SPECIAL LITTLE HUMANS IN MY LIFE THAT HAVE TO GROW UP NAVIGATING A DIGITAL WORLD: EMERSON, LINCOLN, KAI, MILO, SOFIA — B.M.*

*TO VINITA, MY WIFE, LIFE PARTNER AND ENDLESS SOURCE OF SUPPORT — L.H.*

*TO MY PRECIOUS LITTLE ONE, MAY YOU ALWAYS FIND THE STRENGTH TO SAY NO TO DISTRACTIONS AND EMBRACE THE BEAUTY OF THE PRESENT MOMENT — L.B.*

# MAGIC CAT PUBLISHING

10 Steps to Change: How to Say No to Your Phone © 2024 Lucky Cat Publishing Ltd
Text © 2024 Brad Marshall and Lindsay Hassock
Illustrations by Lauriane Bohémier
First Published in 2024 by Magic Cat Publishing, an imprint of Lucky Cat Publishing Ltd, Unit 2 Empress Works, 24 Grove Passage, London E2 9FQ, UK

The rights of Brad Marshall and Lindsay Hassock to be identified as the authors of this work has been asserted by them in accordance with the Copyright, Designs and Patents Act, 1988 (UK).

A catalogue record for this book is available from the British Library.

ISBN 978-1-915569-11-0

The illustrations were created digitally
Set in Cherry, Wisely and Wilden

Published by Rachel Williams and Jenny Broom
Designed by Maisy Ruffels
Edited by Helen Brown

Printed in Dubai

9 8 7 6 5 4 3 2 1

# Contents

# Let's begin by calling out the elephant in the room. Phones are not bad.

They offer convenient ways to communicate with our friends and family. They help to capture and share our important moments and we can use them to relax and have fun, all on something we can fit in our pockets. The challenge is, when something can do all that and it is present all of the time, it can quickly consume our lives.

We're psychologists who are passionate about helping young people and their families tackle the challenge of having a healthy and balanced relationship with technology. At the Screens & Gaming Disorder Clinic in Sydney, Australia, we work with young people who are struggling to manage how they use their devices, to the point that it becomes an addiction. They say things like:

*I FEEL ANXIOUS WHEN I DON'T HAVE MY PHONE WITH ME.*

*RUNNING OUT OF BATTERY ON MY PHONE WOULD FRIGHTEN ME.*

I SEEM TO LOSE TRACK OF TIME WHEN I'M ON MY PHONE.

I'M TIRED BECAUSE I WAKE UP IN THE MIDDLE OF THE NIGHT TO CHECK MY PHONE.

We're not surprised to hear this. Sometimes it can get to the point where it feels like instead of you controlling your phone, your phone is controlling *you*. This can lead to difficulties at home with family, in the playground with friends, or in the classroom at school. We help young people understand why these things happen and we give them skills and strategies to take back control.

This book is a collection of our first-hand knowledge of what we know works and the science that backs it up. Technology is here to stay, whether we like it or not, so let's work to be empowered by devices like our phones, rather than be hindered by them.

**By learning and putting into practice the steps in this book you're kickstarting your journey to a healthy relationship with your phone.**

# What's the problem with our phones?

Phones have found a way to intertwine themselves with our existence. That's not necessarily a negative thing. And it's in no way intended to come across as judgemental.

When we're away from family and friends, keeping in touch via a phone can be a lifesaver. Through social media, instant messaging apps and phone calls we can reach out to others and keep in contact even when we aren't physically together.

However, despite their many pluses, **phones can become all-consuming**. Even when we don't need them, we can find ourselves keeping them close and checking them frequently. Why do we do this?

> THE APPS ON YOUR PHONE ARE SPECIFICALLY DESIGNED TO KEEP YOU AS ENGAGED AS POSSIBLE, FOR AS LONG AS POSSIBLE.

So, if you do find yourself reaching for your phone all the time, or feeling nervous when it's far away from you, don't take it as a sign of weakness. Mobile phone and social media companies spend millions of pounds to hook you in and keep you coming back for more.

**The good news is we can still take charge of our relationship with our phone and make it a healthy one.**

# How do our phones affect us?

Research suggests that our phones have altered almost everything about human life, from the way we sit, speak and think to the way we communicate with each other and collect and give out information.

The first smartphone was invented over two decades ago and so it is not yet clear what the long-term effects are on the brain, but **health experts are concerned that excessive use can be harmful – especially to brains like yours that are not yet fully developed.**

When phones give off sounds and notifications, it triggers the primitive 'fight-or-flight' response that keeps your brain in a state of continual arousal, which is very stressful. As a result, you may notice you become increasingly forgetful, distracted and have difficulty concentrating and finishing tasks, which can lead to feeling frustration and having lower self-esteem.

*THE AVERAGE TEENAGER SPENDS AROUND 7.5 HOURS ON THEIR PHONE EACH DAY, AND TWEENS AGED EIGHT TO TWELVE SPEND ABOUT 4.5 HOURS.*

And the more time we spend looking at a screen, the less time we spend interacting in person with the people we love. This makes it more difficult to establish connections and strong relationships, which are important for our mental health.

# Why are phones so hard to put down?

**Have you ever had that moment of panic when your phone is down to 1% battery and you don't have a charger? Or — gasp! — you've left your phone at home?**

Well, firstly, it's not just you! We've been there. Both the device and all of the apps on them use all sorts of nifty tricks to make us want to keep using our phones as much as possible.

For some people this can lead to an addiction. This is when, despite attempts to stop or limit phone or device use, we begin to see it impact other parts of our lives, including relationships, education or work, and how we're feeling. If this is you, don't worry! We will take you through the signs to watch out for, and show you how you can have a healthier relationship with your phone. **Putting down your phone to pick up this book is a brilliant first step.**

*TO CONTROL YOUR LIFE, CONTROL WHAT YOU PAY ATTENTION TO.*

Today more and more people are waking up to the effects that our phones have on our mental health. They're looking for ways to regain control and break their habits. It's possible, and we can do it... together!

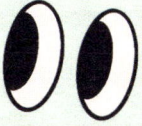

# Level Up Your Knowledge

*HOW MUCH DO YOU TRULY KNOW ABOUT YOUR SMARTPHONE?*

*DO YOU KNOW WHAT IT WANTS FROM YOU? YOUR ATTENTION? YOUR TIME? YOUR MONEY?*

As with all technology, smartphones can have their pros and cons, depending on how they are used. At their best, they can be useful tools for finding out new information. At worst, they can negatively affect our concentration and sleep.

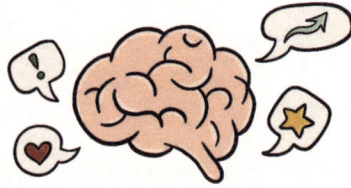

# How do smartphones influence our behaviour?

In 2009, a smart professor called Dr B.J. Fogg came up with a recipe for human behaviour that helps us understand our actions and what drives us to do things. He recognised that there are three ingredients that contribute to a person being much more likely to carry out a certain behaviour.

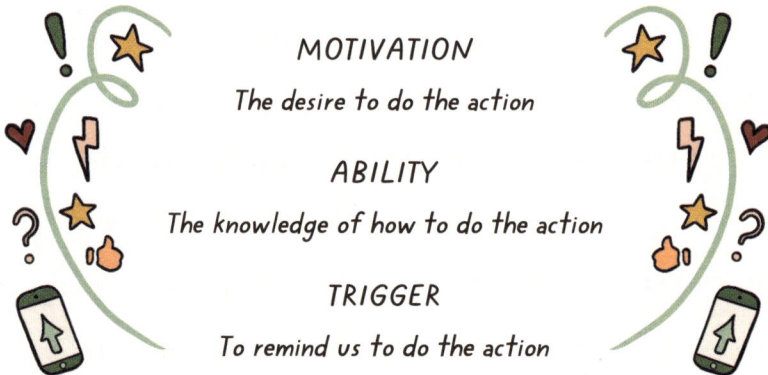

### MOTIVATION
The desire to do the action

### ABILITY
The knowledge of how to do the action

### TRIGGER
To remind us to do the action

Dr Fogg set up a behaviour design laboratory at America's famous Stanford University to teach other people his recipe for human behaviour. There, he taught people who went on to create and lead massive social media companies such as Facebook and Instagram. They used Dr Fogg's recipe to make their apps addictive or what some in the industry call 'sticky': **the more we use our phones, the more money the companies make.**

**Motivation** is the first ingredient needed to make us addicted to our phones. One of the ways apps and technology products keep us coming back is by turning otherwise boring activities into games. This is called gamification. If you use the messaging app Snapchat then you'll be familiar with the 'streaks' that build up when you and a friend send each other snaps over consecutive days. This encourages you to send a daily 'snap' to your friend, so you don't lose your streak, even if you didn't have anything to send a snap about.

*YOUR MOBILE PHONE'S APPS ARE DESIGNED TO CONTROL HOW YOU RESPOND TO THEM.*

**Ability** is the second ingredient. Dr Fogg uses the word to mean how simple it is for someone to do something at a particular moment in time. Think of your favourite video game. Chances are it has a tutorial that introduces you to the game, the characters and how to play. Without this, most people would give up on a game pretty quickly because it would be too confusing. Tutorials include different stages, introducing the most important information first and then adding in more and more information bit by bit.

For example, to start, the game might teach you how to move and navigate the in-game world. Then it might introduce the basic object of the game or simple combat mechanics. Then finally it might teach you how to do a combo or special move that requires pressing several buttons in the right order. So, these days most apps and devices provide tutorials, gradually showing off the features, how to use them, and often even giving rewards or achievements the first time you go through all the different features.

A **trigger** is the third ingredient. How does your phone let you know when there is something new for you to look at? That's right, it sends a push notification that comes with its own 'ding', vibration, a lit-up screen, or even all three! While this can be a useful way to be told when something important happens, it can also be pretty difficult to ignore when we might have more important stuff going on.

*HAVE YOU EVER RECEIVED A NOTIFICATION AND THOUGHT, 'OH, I'VE JUST GOT TO RESPOND TO THIS ONE MESSAGE!', THEN YOU START CHECKING YOUR OTHER SOCIAL MEDIA APPS OR GAMES AND BEFORE YOU KNOW IT YOU'VE LOST TRACK OF TIME?*

If an app on your phone is having trouble getting you, or others, to adopt a certain behaviour, the people designing the app may ask: Is there a motivation problem? If so, how can I fix it? Is there an ability problem? How can I make the behaviour easier or simpler? Am I using the right trigger? Am I applying the trigger at the right time? **Apps target our attention. This is a big deal, because our attention is the most valuable thing we have.**

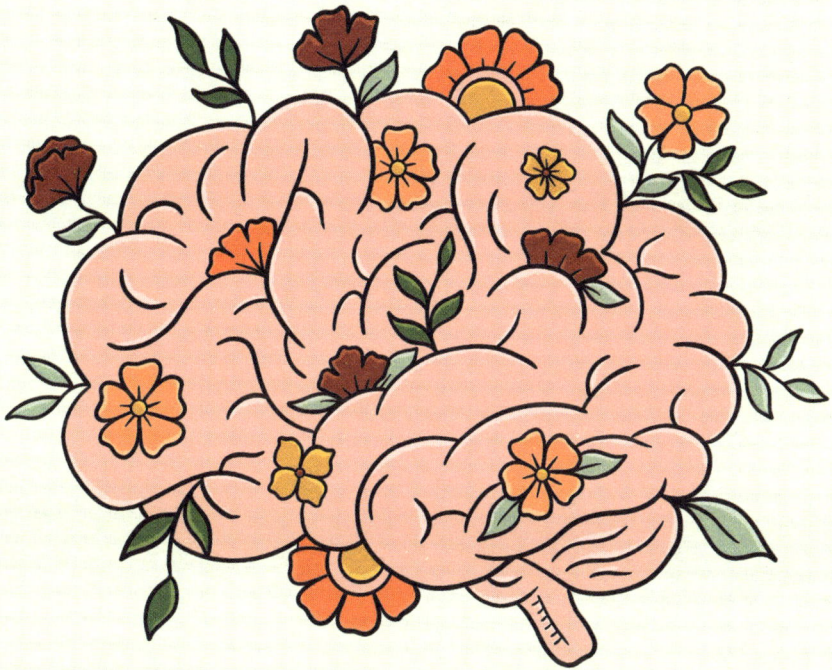

KNOWLEDGE

IS POWER

## Your smartphone stats

Here is a list of questions we'd like you to answer as
best you can.

🌸    How much time do you spend using
your phone each day?

🌸    How many times do you check your
phone each day?

🌸    Which apps do you spend the most
time using?

🌸    Which apps do you tend to
open first?

🌸    Which apps send you notifications?
How often does this happen?

🌸    How quickly do you respond when you
get a notification?

We'd now like you to check your answers against
the reality. You could measure yourself, or ask
your caregivers to measure to you.

You'll start to notice patterns in your behaviour.
How do your statistics compare to the rest of
the world?

## The world's smartphone stats

**4.8H**

THE AVERAGE TIME A PERSON SPENDS ON THEIR PHONE EACH DAY IS **4.8 HOURS.**

58 /day

ON AVERAGE, PEOPLE PICK UP AND OPEN THEIR PHONES **58 TIMES** A DAY.

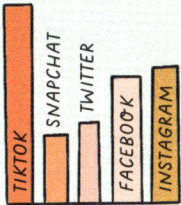

TIKTOK · SNAPCHAT · TWITTER · FACEBOOK · INSTAGRAM

USERS WORLDWIDE SPEND AN AVERAGE OF **95 MINUTES** PER DAY ON TIKTOK.

This is more than four times the average duration spent on Snapchat (21 minutes), over three times the time spent on Twitter (29 minutes) and nearly twice as much as Facebook (49 minutes) and Instagram (51 minutes).

46

THE AVERAGE SMARTPHONE USER IN AMERICA GETS OVER **46 NOTIFICATIONS** A DAY FROM APPS.

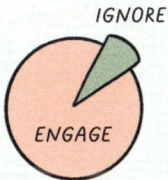

IGNORE · ENGAGE

ONLY 8% OF PEOPLE IGNORE PUSH NOTIFICATIONS. THAT MEANS THAT **92% OF USERS** ENGAGE WITH NOTIFICATIONS IN SOME WAY.

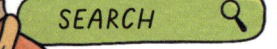

## ⋛ Step 2 ⋛

# Reassess the Relationship

*DO YOU EVER FEEL LOST WHEN YOU DON'T HAVE YOUR PHONE WITH YOU?*

*HAVE YOU FELT PANICKY AS YOUR PHONE BATTERY DIES?*

When our devices become such an important part of our lives that they make us feel negatively when we're without them, then it's time we reassess the relationship. First, it's useful to explore how our relationship with our phones came to be.

# Phones can make us feel good.

How so? Look no further than your own brain and a natural chemical called **dopamine**. This chemical is produced by the brain and makes us feel good whenever we do something we enjoy, like hanging out with our friends, or eating our favourite food. **When we feel good doing these activities, it makes us want to do them again in the future.**

The tricky thing about dopamine, is that we can get a 'hit' (a release of the chemical in the brain) just by having a signal of something good to come, like the smell of our favourite food cooking.

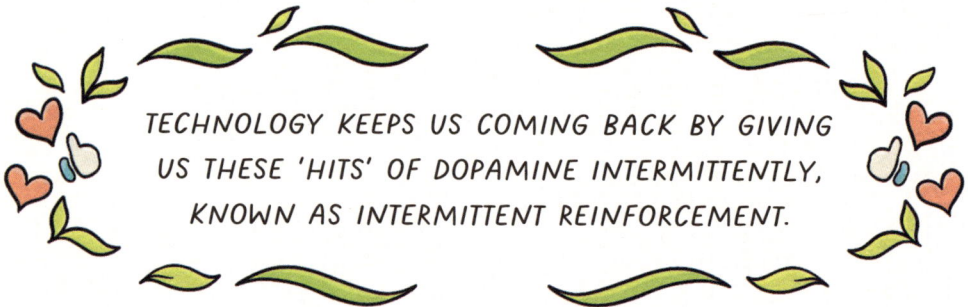

*TECHNOLOGY KEEPS US COMING BACK BY GIVING US THESE 'HITS' OF DOPAMINE INTERMITTENTLY, KNOWN AS INTERMITTENT REINFORCEMENT.*

A great example of this is how every time you check your phone, you have the chance of seeing a new message from your best friend, or maybe even your crush. Then it becomes tempting to keep checking your phone just in case there is something exciting waiting for you.

Do you ever almost beat a level in a mobile phone game and think to yourself, 'That was so close, I bet I'll get it on this next go'? **That's called the 'near-miss effect', and it's an example of intermittent reinforcement that makes us want to keep pursuing goals that feel just out of reach.** By adjusting the difficulty based on your skill level using artificial intelligence (AI), games can make close losses feel like a win.

Another way companies use this is through loot boxes, which are mystery bundles of virtual items related to a video game. Like one of those coin-operated machines at the arcade, they show us just how close we got to the thing we wanted. This makes us think, 'If I just open one more box, I'm sure to get it!', even though the chances of unlocking the item haven't changed.

*THE **OPPORTUNITY** FOR REWARD IS OFTEN JUST AS POWERFUL A MOTIVATOR AS THE REWARD ITSELF.*

This motivator can mean we lose track of time while engrossed in an important group message or new game. This happens when the task grabs our attention and challenges us at the same time — it is called being in a 'state of flow'. This can occur when playing sport, or eating your favourite food (remember those dopamine-producing activities?). It's when you're 'in the zone'. While this can be invaluable when focusing on important activities, it can make it hard to draw your attention away from your phone.

Now let's think about accessibility. Smartphones are so compact we can take them everywhere with us, which is super convenient, right? But have you ever felt like you weren't being listened to by your friend because they were staring at their phone while you were speaking? It can be easy to take out your phone whenever there's a dull moment. This can quickly lead to feeling like you're always multi-tasking and never able to give anything your full attention. The ability to connect with your loved ones anywhere and anytime is incredible. The downside of this is that it can be tricky to ignore, and if we aren't responding it can feel like we are missing out, or create feelings of worry that others don't think you care enough to reply.

Often it appears like the adverts we see on our phones were made just for us. **This happens because technology companies collect data on us based on every interaction we have with our phone, from what content we like to watch to our search history and what apps we use.** They can even track who we are in close proximity to and can see our location.

You may have wondered why lots of the biggest apps like Instagram, TikTok and Facebook don't cost anything. Well, that's because even though you're the one using the app, you aren't their customer. The advertisers are. Those apps make money by charging the advertisers a fee to be able to put a targeted advert right in front of your face.

**When you understand the strategies being used to grab your attention, then you can begin to mount your counterattack!**

GIVE YOURSELF SPACE TO GROW A NEW RELATIONSHIP WITH YOUR PHONE

# Phone addiction quiz

How much do you agree or disagree with the statements below in relation to your smartphone use in the last twelve months?

♥ My phone is the most important thing in my life.

♥ I have had fights with my family or friends because of my phone use.

♥ Using my phone is a way of changing my mood, i.e. I get a buzz, or I can escape or get away.

♥ Over time, I fiddle around more and more with my phone.

♥ If I cannot use or access my phone when I feel like it, I feel sad, moody or irritable.

♥ If I try to cut down on the time I use my phone, I manage to do so for a while, but then I end up using it as much or more than before.

If you found yourself agreeing with any of the statements, then that's a warning signal to reassess your relationship with your phone.

**Good news is that we've got the tools for you to do that right here!**

# How to build a better relationship with your phone

### PRACTISE SCREEN-FREE TIME

Being without your phone for a while each day can reduce the anxiety you feel when you don't have access to it. Before you know it, you'll feel more comfortable without it.

### WATCH OUT FOR THE DOPAMINE HITS

Catch yourself checking your phone unnecessarily, and ask yourself, 'What was I hoping to find?' You might be surprised how often the answer to this is, 'Nothing!'

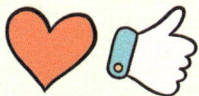

### INTERRUPT THE FLOW

Set a timer for yourself before you begin your game or activity. This can help you to keep track of time and break out of the 'state of flow'.

### SWITCH OFF NOTIFICATIONS

Turning notifications off can reduce the temptation to respond to every message.

### BE MINDFUL OF ADVERTS

Remember that apps make money by charging the advertisers a fee to be able to put an advert in front of your face. When you see an advert, ask yourself, 'Would I have wanted to buy this if it wasn't advertised to me?' If this answer is yes, make a note of the item and wait a week to check if you still want it.

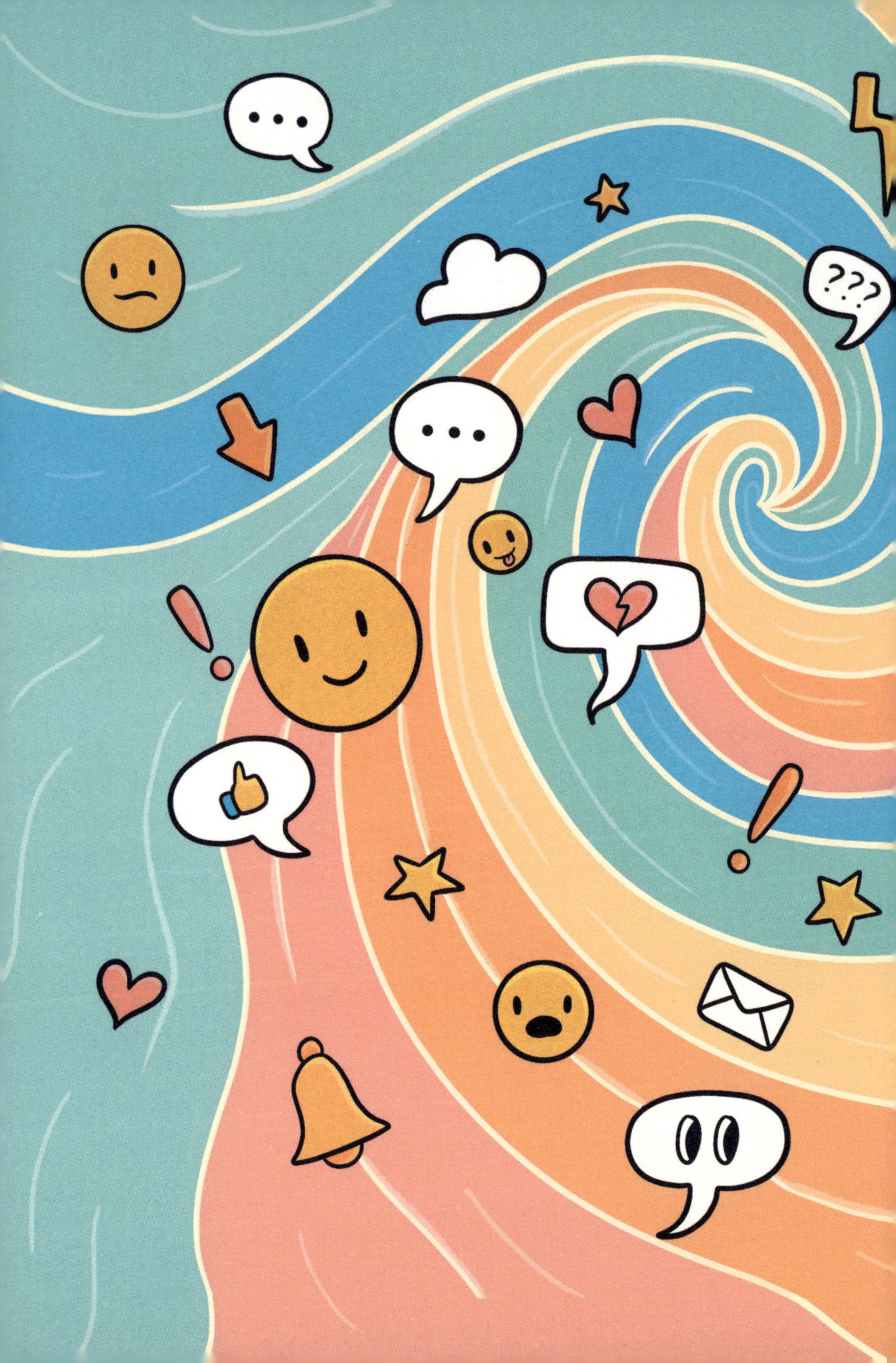

# End the Cycle of Doom

HAVE YOU FOUND YOURSELF MINDLESSLY SCROLLING THROUGH ONE BAD NEWS STORY AFTER ANOTHER?

OR FLICKING THROUGH DISTURBING VIDEOS THAT DON'T INTEREST YOU BUT YOU CAN'T STOP?

What you're experiencing is called 'doomscrolling'. It's so common that the Oxford English Dictionary named it a word of the year in 2020! Unsurprisingly it can be harmful to your mental and physical health.

# It's easy to spend time getting lost down the negative-news rabbit hole.

Wanting to stay informed by keeping up with what's trending locally and around the world is perfectly normal. This helps you know what's happening, so you can learn new information and adjust for the future. **The challenge is that this part of your brain has evolved to have a bias towards negative stuff.** Why? Part of your brain is designed to keep you safe, and to do this, it prioritises watching out for threats.

*WHEN THERE ARE ISSUES LIKE GLOBAL PANDEMICS AND CLIMATE CHANGE BEING WRITTEN AND SPOKEN ABOUT EVERY DAY, IT'S EASY TO FEEL DOOMED.*

The issue of doomscrolling is magnified, too, by the fact that more negative news is published and talked about. News companies and content creators have realised that people are more likely to read and watch their feed if it's negative (because of our bias towards threats), so to increase the number of viewers they produce more and more news on worrying topics.

This gets made even worse by 'clickbait' stories, which gives the article or video an extreme-sounding title like: 'Why the world is going to explode!' This causes the threat-assessment part of your brain to go into overdrive and the temptation to click on that link becomes almost impossible to resist. It makes a lot of sense to want to know if the world is going to explode, right? What if that article was actually about the fact that Earth will be consumed by the Sun in seven to eight billion years (long after your lifetime!) and if humans are still around by then, it's likely they'll have figured out a way to travel far away?

There are two reasons we can get stuck scrolling for more news or information. Firstly, we are seeking out more information.

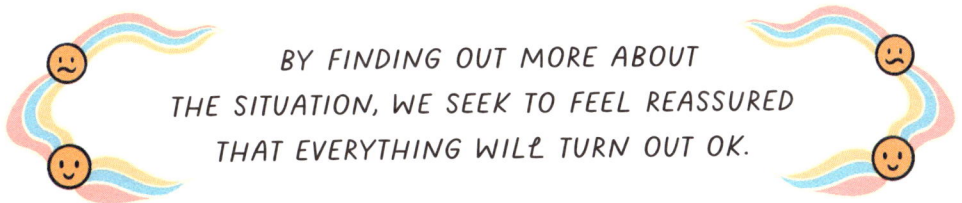

BY FINDING OUT MORE ABOUT THE SITUATION, WE SEEK TO FEEL REASSURED THAT EVERYTHING WILL TURN OUT OK.

However, often this only leads to needing more and more reassurance as the list of problems grow. The second reason we get stuck scrolling negative news is that we want to find a positive news story to counteract all the negativity and bring us a sense of hope. However, while looking for positive news we are bombarded with more and more negative news stories.

These actions mean our biological warning system is in a constant state of high alert, which leads us to feeling stressed out and worn down. Your brain's warning system is designed to trigger a fight-or-flight response, that is to protect yourself or remove yourself from the danger. However, this is difficult to do when the problem is completely outside of your control. As a result, you might experience a 'freeze response' and feel stuck or helpless. Experiencing this all the time can even increase our likelihood of experiencing anxiety or depression.

The trap of doomscrolling has become even easier to fall into because of 'short-form content', like TikTok or YouTube shorts. Having videos capped to sixty seconds means that we only ever get a brief overview of the information and to find out more you have to keep scrolling for the next video. These videos also don't feel like a big investment of our time. **It's easy to keep scrolling when we think, 'Oh, it's only sixty seconds'. Before you know it many minutes or even hours have gone by.** Imagine if each of those videos were five, ten or even thirty minutes. Then you would probably take more time to consider if you could fit in another video before you started.

Learning is a good thing — that's what they encourage in school, right? We just need to make sure it's not leading to us feeling overwhelmed or trapped. To do this we can counteract mindless scrolling, with mindful scrolling. **Mindfulness is about being in the present moment and living our lives according to what truly matters to us. That means being switched on and listening to our own thoughts and feelings.** This means we can catch ourselves if we become worried by an article, or feel disengaged with the videos we're watching. When we notice feelings of worry or disengagement, it's time to give ourselves the break we deserve.

FEELING
OVERWHELMED IS
A SIGN FROM YOUR
BRAIN THAT IT'S TIME
TO GIVE YOURSELF
A BREAK FROM
YOUR PHONE

## Ten tips to combat doomscrolling

### ALLOCATE A TIME LIMIT

By setting yourself a window of time to read websites or watch videos, you give yourself a way to stop the cycle at the end of your time.

### SET BOUNDARIES ON CONTENT

If there are certain apps that you find particularly difficult to manage yourself or topics that you find triggering, set your own limits. After all, you know yourself best.

### ENGAGE WITH CHEERY CONTENT

Engage with content that aligns with topics that you are passionate about, like your hobbies. This keeps your phone use as a tool that supports you, rather than you supporting it!

### TAKE A DEEP BREATH

When you notice yourself feeling overwhelmed or becoming stuck in a cycle, stop for a second and take one deep breath. Often this will be enough to allow you to slow down, and do the next step...

### CHECK IN WITH YOURSELF

If you are feeling stressed, upset or agitated, that's a good sign it's time to get off your phone and do something else to relax.

## ASK YOURSELF 'WHY'?

By asking yourself why you're currently scrolling, you might notice that instead of doing it to enjoy yourself, you're doomscrolling to avoid thinking about or doing something else.

## MANAGE NOTIFICATIONS

By only having notifications for important apps and keeping distracting apps off your home screen, you can avoid checking your phone regularly and being tempted into scrolling when you do need to check your phone.

## MANAGE FUTURE WORRIES

If you find yourself worrying about what might happen in the future based on some of the information you're reading, try focusing on the present moment and all the positives that are occurring in your life right now.

## PRACTISE GRATITUDE

List three things that you are grateful for each day. This helps to train your brain to notice the positives and not become so focused on the negative.

## BE KIND TO YOURSELF

We all slip up sometimes. If you catch yourself having fallen into a doomscroll, instead of beating yourself up for it, praise yourself for catching it and use that to break the cycle next time.

# Understand Your Emotions

OUR EMOTIONS ARE ALWAYS PRESENT.

THEY CAN INFLUENCE ALL KINDS OF BEHAVIOUR, INCLUDING HOW LIKELY WE ARE TO USE OUR PHONE AND FOR WHAT PURPOSE.

Whilst phones can be a convenient tool to distract ourselves from our unpleasant emotions, we often find that this is not only unsuccessful in the long run but we can end up with even more feelings of stress, anxiety and sadness.

# Where do our emotions come from? Why do we have them?

We hear these two questions all the time in our clinic. The first thing we tell people is that as a child, teenager and even a young adult, **your brain should come with a sign that says: 'still downloading'!**

Your brain is made up of a number of important parts and one of the last ones to fully develop is called the 'prefrontal cortex' (the section at the very front of your brain just behind your eyes and forehead). This area's job is to help us plan ahead, make important decisions and practise self-control. If you find any of these hard, that's perfectly normal. For most people the prefrontal cortex doesn't finish developing until our mid-20s.

Don't worry, that doesn't mean that you must wait until you're twenty-five or even thirty before it starts doing its job. It's already working, but it's just going to take some time to improve at its job. Think of it as when you first learned to write: you had to learn how to hold a pencil, how much pressure to use, what shapes make letters and what letters make words, but with practice you mastered that skill. It wasn't like you just woke up one morning and knew how to write. Your prefrontal cortex is doing the same.

We like to think of it as your brain going through a 'pruning' process. Imagine that your brain is an overgrown garden full of flowers and weeds. These are all the bits of information your brain has absorbed as a younger child. As you grow up, your brain is becoming more efficient at deciding what are the 'flowers' and what are the 'weeds'.

*YOUR BRAIN LABELS ANY PART THAT IS BEING USED OFTEN AS A 'FLOWER', AS IT MUST BE USEFUL IF YOU'RE USING IT, WHILE THE PARTS THAT DON'T GET USED OFTEN ARE LABELLED 'WEEDS', AND TRIMMED BACK.*

**This is why it's important to keep trying new things and making sure you stick with stuff even if it feels hard at first.**

Since the prefrontal cortex is still downloading, a part of the brain you rely on more is called the 'limbic system', in particular the 'amygdala'. This area of the brain is buried deep in towards the centre of the brain, and it's the centre of our emotions. Remember the flight-or-flight response from the last step? This is the region of the brain that's responsible for it!

As the amygdala is designed to keep us safe, it is impulsive and encourages instinctive behaviour (acting before thinking) when we feel strong emotions like fear. This is extremely useful when you might be in a life-or-death situation and don't have time to think things through.

Thankfully, most of the time we aren't in a situation where our life is in danger. However, the amygdala is sensitive and can jump into action even when it isn't needed. If you've ever reacted based on emotions, then you have your amygdala to thank. The limbic system is also sensitive to rewards. Does that ring a bell? Rewards are exactly what our old friend dopamine is all about.

It is natural to want to soothe ourselves when we feel emotional. A common trap for doing this is with sugary food. The reason this works is that sugar lowers our stress levels temporarily while giving us a big hit of dopamine. This reward makes us want to do this again the next time we're experiencing intense emotions. In this way, sugar can become addictive. Using your phone to calm yourself when emotional is no different.

*BY PAYING ATTENTION TO OUR EMOTIONS, WE HAVE A BETTER CHANCE AT **ACTING** IN A WAY WE WANT TO, INSTEAD OF **REACTING** IN A WAY OUR EMOTIONS WANT US TO.*

**Your emotions are there for a reason and there is nothing wrong with them, even the difficult ones.** By paying attention to them, you can pick up on what they are telling you and let yourself process that important message. Otherwise, we end up using devices like our phones to distract ourselves. Because our phones are so entertaining, we can avoid or dull our emotions while we are using them. But the long-term problem is that the emotions are still waiting for us when we disconnect.

MUCH LIKE A
COMPASS THAT
GUIDES US IN THE
RIGHT DIRECTION,
EMOTIONS HAVE
THE POWER TO
GUIDE US TO THE
RIGHT ACTIONS

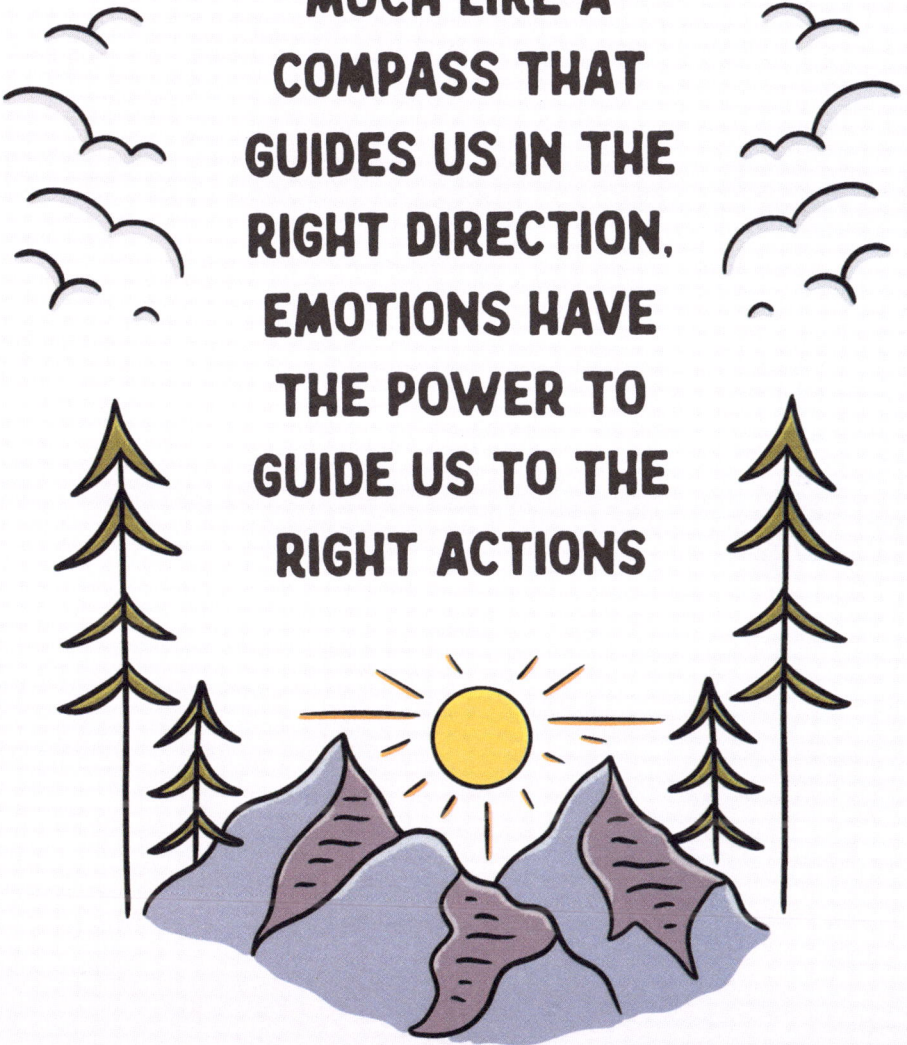

# Emotion regulation skills

If you find yourself using your smartphone as a 'security blanket' to manage your feelings, try...

### CREATING SPACE

Emotions happen fast. So the gift we can give ourselves is to pause. Take a breath. Slow down the moment between trigger and response.

### NOTICING YOUR BODY

Tune in to your body. Is your stomach upset? Is your heart racing? Your physical symptoms can be clues to what is happening emotionally.

### NAMING HOW YOU FEEL

Many of us feel more than one emotion at a time, so don't hesitate to identify multiple emotions. Then dig deeper. If you feel fear, what are you afraid of? Being able to name your feelings will help you share your emotions with others.

### ACCEPTING HOW YOU FEEL

Emotions are a normal part of how we respond to situations. Practise self-compassion and treat yourself like you would a friend.

### PRACTISING MINDFULNESS

Mindfulness helps us 'live in the moment' by paying attention to what is inside us. Use your senses to notice what is happening around you. These skills can help you stay calm and avoid engaging in negative thought patterns.

# Dealing with emotions head-on

## POSITIVE AFFIRMATIONS

Saying short, positive daily statements such as, 'I can do this' will help you feel stronger and more able to cope with challenging situations.

## JOURNALLING

Writing down how you feel helps to get it out of your head and on to paper. This frees up your mental space and helps you relieve the stress of the emotions you've been carrying around.

## TALKING IT OUT

Having a trusted person who you can talk to about how you're feeling is helpful in making sure you don't feel alone and you have an outlet to talk about your feelings.

## EDUCATE YOURSELF

There is plenty of content out there to help you educate yourself on the emotion you are dealing with. Knowledge and understanding can help you feel empowered to make changes when needed.

## SPEND TIME OUTDOORS

Being outside is beneficial for our mental health. Even something as simple as watching the birds has a calming effect.

# Build New Habits

*IS THERE A BEHAVIOUR THAT YOU DO OVER AND OVER AGAIN, ALMOST WITHOUT THINKING?*

*PERHAPS IT'S SCROLLING ON YOUR PHONE BEFORE BED, OR WHEN YOU'RE ON THE TOILET.*

This behaviour is known as a habit, and the truth is, when you've been doing something the same way for weeks, months or even years, then doing something different is going to be difficult. But don't give up! If you keep at it, you can turn new behaviours into habits, too.

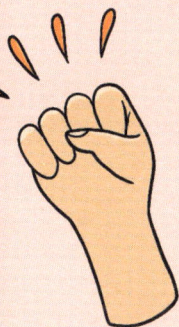

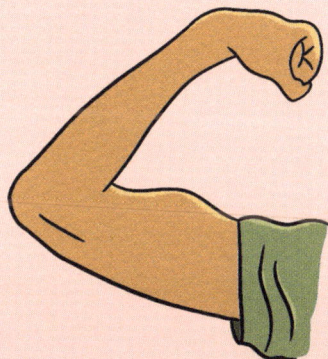

# Habits form through a process known as the habit loop.

There are three elements that work together to form a habit.

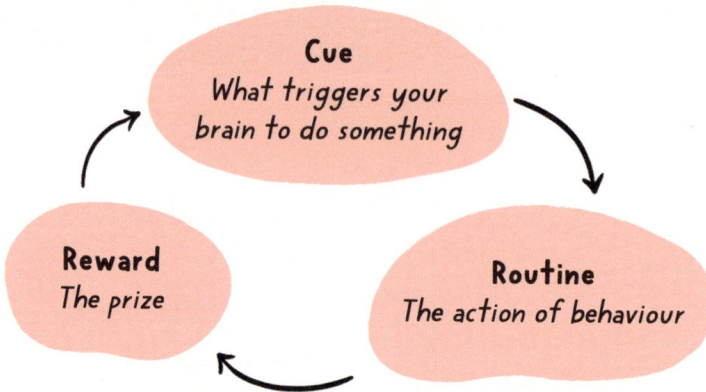

**Cue**
*What triggers your brain to do something*

**Routine**
*The action of behaviour*

**Reward**
*The prize*

First up: the **cue!** This is your trigger that encourages the following behaviour. For instance, in the mornings, the ringing of the alarm or your caregivers waking you up is the cue to get the morning routine going. Next, there's the **routine**. Habits aren't just one action that's disconnected from the rest of your actions. What comes before and after the habitual behaviour is part of the habit, whether that's getting out of bed or sitting down on the toilet. Whenever a cue triggers your habit, you'll start following the defined routine that your brain has developed. The **reward** is whatever outcome you achieve. For example, if your habit, using your smartphone, helps you feel emotionally better, that is your reward. This is something that your brain considers to be a positive outcome. Hence, you unconsciously want to repeat the habit again and again to achieve the satisfaction of the reward.

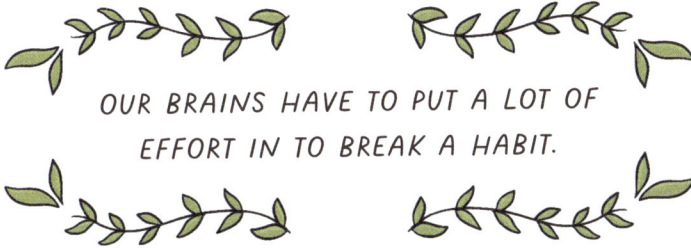

*OUR BRAINS HAVE TO PUT A LOT OF EFFORT IN TO BREAK A HABIT.*

For example, when we can see our phone on the desk at school or on the dinner table, our brains must put in effort just to ignore them. You might have noticed your friend or caregivers glancing over at their phone during a conversation even though it hasn't beeped or buzzed.

So, what can we do? Well, you might have thought about or, even more likely, been told about giving screens up all together. However, this is almost impossible (unless you can change your lifestyle to never come across any screens ever again!)

You might have experienced this when you go on a school trip or a family holiday where you don't have access to your phone. When there is no option or temptation it's easy to 'give it up', and you might have even thought about how nice it was to be away from screens for a while. However, we're guessing that once you came back home, you were right back on to your phone as though nothing had ever changed. Because screens aren't going anywhere, we're constantly reminded that they exist. **When we try and ignore our phones, we actually end up thinking about them**

**even more.** Don't believe us? Picture in your head a big white fluffy polar bear. Now, close your eyes for thirty seconds and try to not think about a big white fluffy polar bear... How did you do? If you're anything like us, you probably thought about the polar bear. This is because we're thinking about something without thinking about the things we're trying to *not* think about. What a confusing sentence, we know. **Instead, what works better is replacing our unwanted habits with alternative, desired habits.**

The first step in the process is to figure out *why* you were doing the unwanted behaviour in the first place. For example, are you using social media to keep connected with friends? Or are you watching YouTube videos because you love learning about new things? Once we know the reason, we can come up with an alternative habit that achieves the same goal but without the drawbacks of getting absorbed by your phone.

Next, we need to set ourselves up for success in starting these new habits. Bad habits tend to repeat themselves not because you don't want to change, but because you have the wrong system for change. Good thing we've already learned the recipe for behaviour back in Step 1 from Professor B.J. Fogg! First up, you need some **motivation** — this could be a desire to connect with your friends in person rather than online. Second, we need the **ability**. Your new habit needs to be easy and achievable, like meeting in the park, rather than hard and unrealistic like meeting at a theme park. Finally, we need a **trigger** — like booking it in with your friends for after school once a week. **When you have successfully established a momentum, you'll be building new habits at a pace that far exceeds your own expectations!**

YOU DON'T BREAK
A BAD HABIT — YOU
REPLACE IT WITH
A GOOD HABIT

## How to build a new habit

If you don't have anything to replace your phone habit with, you'll be pulled towards checking it. Here are some ways to help you build a new habit:

### START SMALL

Start with tiny habits to make the new habit as easy as possible in the beginning. You could spend five minutes drawing before using your phone when you get home.

### DO IT EVERY DAY

Habits form faster when we do them more often, so start with something that is really easy to do, like reading a book before bed every night instead of looking at your phone.

### MAKE IT EASY

We are more likely to form new habits when we clear away the obstacles that stand in our way. Have a board game out ready to play with your family after dinner, whilst keeping your phone out of sight.

### GET A BUDDY

Find someone who will build a new habit with you and keep you motivated. Good habits are contagious so try to catch some by hanging out with people who are a little ahead of you on the learning curve.

## TIE IT TO A TRIGGER

Tie the goal or behaviour you are trying to turn into a habit to something you already do on a regular basis. If you want to journal each day, tie this to an action you already do. For example, each time you get out of the shower, spend a few minutes journalling. This creates a bond between the trigger and new habit so that you'll soon start to do one immediately following the other.

## MAKE IT REWARDING

Pay attention to how good it feels, or use a treat to reward yourself afterwards. You could treat yourself with five minutes of screen time after thirty minutes of reading. Eventually you will enjoy the goal or behaviour without the reward. However, first you need to trick your brain into creating this automatic habit by rewarding yourself first.

## BE REALISTIC

To change a behavior and turn it into a long-lasting habit requires willpower, which is a limited resource. We don't have enough willpower to take on changing several habits at once, so it's important to build one habit at a time. Rome wasn't built in a day!

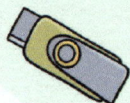

# Switch Off For Success

*DOING WELL AT SCHOOL IS OFTEN
A BIG SOURCE OF STRESS.*

*IT'S EASY TO FEEL PRESSURE FROM
YOUR SCHOOL, YOUR CAREGIVERS
AND EVEN FROM YOURSELF.*

School is where you currently spend over
25% of your time during a typical school
week, and that's without including
homework or extracurricular activities.
Where does your phone use fit into this?
When can it be helpful? And when can it
get in the way of your success?

# Schoolwork can feel like a battleground when technology is involved.

You've probably had an argument with your caregiver about it. In a recent study in Australia, 83% of caregivers think their children are negatively distracted by digital devices. In our experience, caregivers often don't see all of the work young people are doing as well as some of the obstacles getting in the way of doing schoolwork.

Having our phones handy to be able to receive updates and feedback on the fly can seem useful at times, but this can quickly become a constant distraction with notifications from group chats going 'ding, ding, ding' every five seconds. It can feel important to keep our phones on us to make sure that we don't miss out on what's going on in our group chats with friends and we are often waiting for friends to reply to our messages.

*HAVE YOU EVER EXPERIENCED BEING LEFT ON 'READ', WONDERING WHY THEY HAVEN'T YET RESPONDED AND FEELING THE URGE TO SEND ANOTHER MESSAGE TO GET THEM TO RESPOND?*

**This feeling is called the 'Zeigarnik effect', where your brain is better at noticing interruption (such as an unfinished conversation) because it wants a logical conclusion.** If a friend has seen your message, but not responded to it, your brain starts going haywire trying to figure out why they haven't responded. In reverse the 'read' feature can even result in you feeling guilty for not replying to a friend after you get a message from them. This encourages a constant cycle of messages, even if you don't have much to talk about. **Social media apps have realised how effective the 'read' feature is for keeping people using their apps — they don't even offer the option to turn this feature off!** This can make it really difficult for your brain to concentrate on anything else, like your homework.

We hear children in our clinic say that quite often their homework takes them way longer than their teachers say it should. This is usually because they have chat windows open or they have their phone next to their laptop with the notifications switched on, so they are essentially trying to multitask. It can be really helpful to sit down with your caregivers or teachers and explain what you find easy, what you're finding more challenging, the steps you're taking to get things done, and what help you need, if any. **Often adults become nosier when they feel like they're being kept out of the loop, but if you involve them you can take steps to success together.**

After all, technology can actually contribute to learning at school. In 2022, a secondary school in New Zealand trialled a 'bring your own device' initiative. Pupils were encouraged to bring their smartphones to use in class. The school found that the students' digital skills improved and there were increased opportunities for collaboration both between pupils and between pupils and teachers.

Schools around the world embraced technology as a whole during the COVD-19 pandemic, too. This made remote learning possible, keeping everyone's education going during lockdowns and maintaining relationships with school friends and teachers. Schools realised that technology provides lots of opportunities for creative learning by making dull tasks more fun and giving chances to create digital content. For a lot of students this has helped them to engage in classes they may not like, find new areas of learning and gain skills that prepare them for working in the modern world.

Today, even though most schools ban the use of smartphones, classrooms are still full of screens, from laptops to tablets. This makes it hard to be screen-free, and can even extend into time at home as schools are increasingly using online portals for communicating with their students. While this can be handy to have all of the information for school in one place it means that school tasks are given via these online portals and are expected to be submitted in a digital format. **No wonder it's hard to switch off!**

To find balance, we must acknowledge and embrace the value of technology when used productively in a classroom setting to maximise learning, whilst managing the potent distractions our phones can be when we're trying to concentrate on our schoolwork.

*WHEN WE SET GUIDELINES FOR HOW WE USE OUR PHONE, WE CAN AVOID FALLING INTO THE TRAPS THAT ROB US OF OUR CONCENTRATION.*

# What personality are you?

## The Procrastinator

You find yourself scrolling or gaming when you're meant to be completing schoolwork.

*WHY THIS HAPPENS*

Homework can feel really overwhelming, which can make it tempting to delay starting or completing.

*WHAT TO DO*

Break your work down into manageable parts. Set yourself small goals to get yourself started and feel a sense of achievement.

## The Perfectionist

You spend endless hours researching information on the internet or confirming answers with your friends.

*WHY THIS HAPPENS*

Perfectionism can lead to unrelenting standards that you place on yourself because the fear of being 'wrong' or 'not good enough' is unbearable.

*WHAT TO DO*

Try to keep the focus on process rather than outcome. Do schoolwork offline where possible. Reduce temptations by keeping your phone out of reach and eyesight.

## The Rebel

You find yourself exploring other interests on your phone that fall outside what's being delivered in the school curriculum, and will question the purpose of almost everything.

*WHY THIS HAPPENS*

Some people find traditional academic learning dull or difficult and prefer focusing on the topics that naturally interest them.

*WHAT TO DO*

Use a timer to set regular breaks so you have time to do something you enjoy. A common method is called the Pomodoro Technique, which is twenty-five minutes of concentration then a five-minute break.

## The Forgetter

You enjoy spending your free time on your phone and before you know it you're saying, 'Oh no, I forgot' when it comes to your schoolwork.

*WHY THIS HAPPENS*

Our phones are designed to grab and keep our attention, which makes it easy to forget about important things like schoolwork.

*WHAT TO DO*

Ask for help to receive structure, repetition and reminders. Prioritise your schoolwork and use time on your phone as a reward for when you complete it.

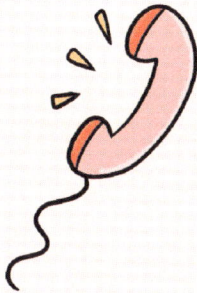

## ≋ Step 7 ≋

# Online vs. Offline Friendships

PHONES ARE A BIG PART OF HOW WE CONNECT WITH OUR FRIENDS.

THE MOST ADDICTIVE SMARTPHONE FUNCTIONS ALL SHARE A COMMON THEME: THEY TAP INTO THE HUMAN DESIRE TO CONNECT TO OTHER PEOPLE.

This can often be why it's so hard to change how we use our phone. But what if every like, heart and reply we give to someone through our phones is actually taking away from our energy for our friendships in real life?

# We admit it: it'll be hard to change how you use your phone when all your friends are still using theirs.

You may feel like you're missing out. As with lots of things, like exercise and studying, it's a lot easier to change our actions as a group than by ourselves. When we see others making a change, this can help to motivate us. It also helps to have someone else to check in on how we're doing with sticking to the change. When we do it on our own it can feel lonely, and this makes changes easier to give up.

*YOU MAY BE SURPRISED HOW MUCH EASIER SAYING NO TO YOUR PHONE WILL BECOME WHEN YOU WORK WITH YOUR FRIENDS.*

We hear a lot about how technology is harming our mental heath, but scientists have found that completely cutting out technology for young people can actually reduce their wellbeing. This is because so many of the opportunities to connect with friends happen online. When these are cut off, it can lead to feeling disconnected.

**However, it is important that online time leads to catching up with our friends face to face, otherwise the benefits are quickly lost.** When we hang out with our friends, our brains produce chemicals that help us feel better both physically and emotionally.

*ONLINE CHATTING CAN'T REPLACE THE JOY OF CATCHING UP WITH FRIENDS IN REAL LIFE.*

Communicating online can sometimes feel more powerful and intimate than when we meet and chat with people face to face. This is called the 'hyperpersonal effect'. We feel like we have a safety barrier when we're online because we're not physically with the people we're communicating with. This means that we feel like we can say things we might not be brave enough to say face to face.

We can form powerful connections with others because of how honest we feel we can be. However, it also means that we are more sensitive to negative feedback from these people we feel overly connected to. This problem becomes magnified when people have a sense of anonymity online, as they are more likely to be unkind because they don't have to experience the consequences of saying those things to another person's face. This can lead to cyberbullying, especially when comments are left anonymously.

**Human beings are social creatures. We're designed to hang out with each other and be in groups rather than alone.**

So, we've evolved to care a lot about what other people think of us and to compare ourselves to others. This is important if you want to fit in, right?

This becomes tricky with social media as we are now able to compare ourselves to others constantly, and not just with our local community, but with the other eight billion people around the planet who also use a smartphone. **Because people tend to only show the good stuff online it can make us feel like there is something wrong with our lives when they don't match what we see online.** Plus, with phone cameras and apps with photo editing software, often what people post online these days is not even a real reflection of their lives. Many influencers have spoken out about the hundreds of photos they will take to get to the one they actually post — and that's even before all the filters and editing happens! When we compare our real lives to the enhanced ones online, it's hard to measure up.

It can be difficult to know how to start a conversation with your friends about phone use. Perhaps you feel pressured to always be online and available, in case your friends are trying to contact you? **But wanting space doesn't make you a bad person, and being constantly available isn't a requirement of being a good friend.** You don't need to say why, but if you wanted to you could say something like, 'I've realised that I need to be more focused in the evening until I finish my homework, which means I won't be able to reply to your message straight away.' Or, to just toss your phone to the side until you can bear the sight of it again — and that becomes easier if you actually take the time to decide when, and why, that is...

A TRUE
FRIEND ACCEPTS
WHO YOU ARE –
AND HELPS YOU
BECOME WHO YOU
SHOULD BE

# Warning signs to look out for to protect your mental health

How much social media connection is too much? Here are a few signs that it's time to log off to improve your mental health:

⭐ You spend more time on social media than you do with friends

⭐ You direct all of your attention towards capturing content for social media, and don't enjoy the experience in real time

⭐ You often compare yourself to your friends and feel jealous of what they are posting

⭐ You experience hurtful harassment such as cyberbullying or trolling

⭐ You find yourself getting caught up in hurtful conversations about others

⭐ You check your social media feed again and again and again so you don't feel out of the loop with what your friends are up to

The most important way to protect your wellbeing is to talk about any concerns you may have about how much you use social media with someone you trust... like your real-life friends!

# How to help your friends with their phone use

Knowing when to go offline can be key for your mental health. It's tempting to help your friends, too. Here are some tips to starting a good conversation:

## *REHEARSE WHAT YOU WANT TO SAY*

Practise scenarios you encounter and how your friends may respond. By communicating assertively, we can maintain respect for them while also acknowledging our own needs. Saying the words aloud will help you make changes, and it'll give you a chance to work on choosing the right words.

## *USE 'I FEEL' STATEMENTS*

Saying things like, 'I feel ignored when you are looking at your phone during our conversations' helps others to understand how their actions might be affecting you.

## *USE FACTS INSTEAD OF JUDGEMENTS*

By saying, 'You often look at your phone when we're talking' instead of, 'You never listen to me' helps to avoid exaggerating the situation and upsetting your friends.

## *CHECK YOUR BODY LANGUAGE*

In addition to what you say, your body language and facial expressions are also important. Act confident even if you aren't feeling it.

# Get Your Family Involved

*TECHNOLOGY HAS BROUGHT NEW CHALLENGES FOR FAMILIES.*

*HOW AND WHEN SCREENS ARE USED CAN LEAD TO FAMILY CONFLICTS.*

Caregivers are often desperate to know how to limit their kids' screen time and young people are fed up with their caregivers trying to control everything about their technology. What if instead of having your caregivers decide for you, you led the charge?

# You're on a journey to becoming your own person.

This is an important time in your life when you're beginning to figure out who you are, what your interests are, what kind of person you want to be, and how you identify. **This is a process called 'individuation', which basically means identifying yourself as a unique person.** To achieve this, you might notice wanting to spend more time with your friends and less time with your family, wanting more privacy, focusing more on yourself and your appearance, and wanting to rebel against your family or culture's expectations. This is one area where phones and the internet have enabled young people to explore themselves with a sense of freedom and privacy. However, this can sometimes lead to problems in relationships with family members.

*ONE CHALLENGE THAT YOUNG PEOPLE OFTEN ACKNOWLEDGE WHEN TRYING TO CHANGE THEIR PHONE USE, IS THAT THEIR CAREGIVERS ARE ON THEIR PHONES JUST AS MUCH – IF NOT MORE – THAN THEY ARE.*

Understandably, it can be hard to take advice from someone who is doing the exact opposite. That's like someone trying to tell you to cut down on the amount of sugar you're eating while stuffing their face with sweets. This can be one of the ways that you may have learnt your phone habits. If your caregiver is frequently checking their phone or always keeps them visible, it's no wonder that you do the same. This is a process called 'modelling', where we learn by copying the actions of those around us.

*A BIG STEP IN CHANGING YOUR OWN PHONE USE MAY BE CHANGING YOUR FAMILY'S.*

**Some families have even forgotten how to spend time together without screens.** Whether it's watching a movie together, or playing video games, these have become easy ways to spend time together as a family because it's so convenient. Don't get us wrong, these can be fun and important family activities and traditions. However, it's important that your family also has shared activities that happen without a screen. Chances are you used to do some of these activities, like playing board games, going to the beach, or walking your dog. We bet you could even come up with some new ones to try together.

To understand why our phones and other screens can cause so many family arguments so easily, lets rewind to the 'state of flow' that we learned about in Step 2. **Phones are so well designed to grab and keep our attention that we often zone out everything else.** This can make it hard to hear what others are saying to us. When this happens, we honestly can't remember what we were told or even that we were told anything.

You might have even experienced this yourself when talking to someone who is on their phone or another device. It feels pretty frustrating when we don't feel listened to, right? **Breaking out of that 'state of flow' is key to improving communication within your family.**

One common opportunity to connect as a family and disconnect from screens is when you break the school/work routine and go on holiday. You might have less access to technology or are busy doing other fun activities, making your phone easy to forget about. Sometimes it can be tempting to try to capture every moment of your holiday to be able to share it with your friends when you return. However, this can impact on your ability to enjoy yourself because you're so focused on getting the best photo. Try using the mindfulness skill of being present and you'll be surprised at how different your experience can be. See what you can notice when you give your full attention to being on holiday.

Now, we're not saying that you should go tech-free every holiday. Screens can be a powerful way to have important shared moments with family members who you might not be able to visit in person. Being able to video call your special family and friends when they are on the other side of the planet is just one example of the benefits of screens. **But we all know by now, even the simple presence of a smartphone — much less its glowing screen and constant beeps — interrupts our ability to connect!**

# How to become your family's screen-time coach

### LOG THE HOURS

If your family members aren't convinced they need time away from their screens, challenge them to keep track of the time they spend on their devices. They might be surprised at how many hours of the day they spend on them!

### SHARE KNOWLEDGE

Sit down with your family and explain what you've learned. If their screen use feels like it's impacting you, let them know politely and explain how modelling works.

### SET SOME GROUND RULES

With your family's permission, you could agree on some digital detox rules. Some of the rules could make use of the functionality of the device itself, while others could be about physically removing yourself from it. Here are some ideas:

⭐ Delete social media apps from your phone.

⭐ Turn off all banner-style/pop-up/sound notifications from other apps.

⭐ Leave your phone in your pocket or keep it out of sight for meals.

## CHALLENGE EACH OTHER

You could try and complete a different test each week, and see how you get on. Here are some ideas:

⭐ **Week 1** Leave your phone outside your bedroom overnight.

⭐ **Week 2** Put your phone in a central place when you return home and go to the location of the phone (rather than carrying it around with you) if you need to check it.

⭐ **Week 3** Keep your phone on airplane mode as default all day; take it off this mode only when you need to use it.

## ORGANISE FAMILY SCREEN-FREE TIME

Brainstorm fun screen-free activities that your family can do together. Pick a few activities from each person's list, and schedule them on the calendar.

Try to come up with a few activities that you can do at home and a few you can do outside so you'll always have some options no matter the weather!

# Have Better Sleep

WE ALL KNOW THAT WE FEEL BETTER
AFTER A GOOD NIGHT'S SLEEP.

BUT WHY EXACTLY IS IT SO
IMPORTANT?

We spend about one-third of our
life sleeping (or attempting to do so!).
Technology can impact how well we sleep,
though, by stimulating our brains.
Mastering the skills to get a good
night's sleep can provide you with
a great foundation to saying no
to your phone.

# Better sleep = better mood!

Sleep helps us in so many ways, from recharging our energy levels to improving our ability to focus. Good sleep can even make us feel happier! Did you know some athletes even sleep for extra periods of time to help them think and react faster and give them a competitive edge?

When we feel rested, we are better able to manage our emotions. Remember in Step 4 we looked at the idea that when we master our emotions we are better able to decide when and how we want to use our phones? **When people regularly don't get enough sleep, this leads them to be more likely to use their phone mindlessly for an easy way to comfort themselves and try to feel better.**

Do you know how much sleep you should be getting each night?

*IF YOU ARE SIX TO TWELVE YEARS OLD YOU NEED NINE TO TWELVE HOURS.*

*IF YOU ARE THIRTEEN TO EIGHTEEN YEARS OLD YOU NEED EIGHT TO TEN HOURS.*

You might be wondering why there is a range of time between the number of hours that is recommended. This is because every person is a little bit different and some might need more than others. The thing to remember is that you should be getting more than the smaller number of hours each night.

There are four ways to tell if you are getting a good night's sleep. Firstly, **are you sleeping for long enough?** The reason this is important is because when we sleep our brain goes through a cycle that takes several hours. We move from **light sleep**, where we're relaxed and drowsy but easy to wake, to **deep sleep**, where our core temperature drops and breathing slows down, to **REM sleep**, which is the dream state that helps with our emotional wellbeing. You might have even noticed these stages if you've ever been woken up while you're super sleepy and it's taken a while for your brain to switch on; or sometimes your brain is super quick to get going. This happens when you get woken up during different parts of your sleep cycle. When we don't get enough sleep we miss out on the most important part of this cycle, which is what helps to recharge our bodies.

Secondly, **do you have a regular bedtime and wake up?** This teaches our body what the routine is and then it knows what to expect.

Thirdly, **can you sleep solid through the night?** Waking up frequently can interrupt our sleep cycle. When you can't get back to sleep quickly, you won't get enough quality sleep to keep you refreshed and healthy.

Lastly, **are you sleeping at night instead of during the day?** This might seem obvious but it's actually super important. Sleeping at night helps align the body's circadian rhythm, or internal clock, with its environment. Proper circadian timing is important for sleep quality.

Don't worry if some or all of your answers to those questions are 'no'! To understand this we first need to explain the role of another important brain chemical: 'melatonin'. Melatonin has an important job of making us sleepy and keeping our sleep and waking routine regular. Our brain makes melatonin when we are in darkness. But our electronic screens produce what is called 'blue light', which is the whiter- or cooler-looking light.

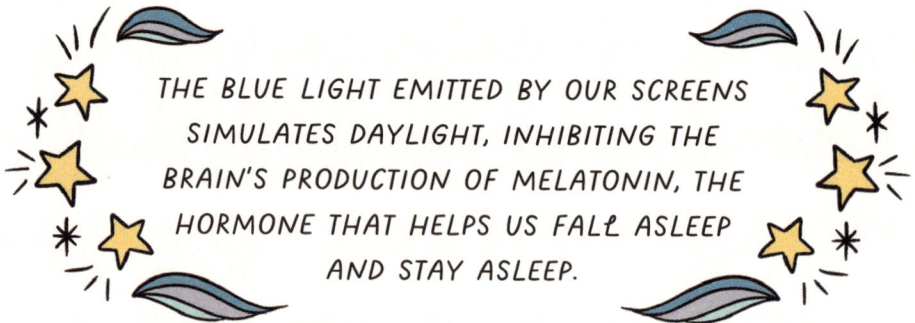

THE BLUE LIGHT EMITTED BY OUR SCREENS SIMULATES DAYLIGHT, INHIBITING THE BRAIN'S PRODUCTION OF MELATONIN, THE HORMONE THAT HELPS US FALL ASLEEP AND STAY ASLEEP.

Also, remember our good old friend (the brain chemical) 'dopamine' from Step 2? Because the activities we do on our screens are so fun, like chatting to our friends, or watching videos, we get a lot of dopamine in our brain. **Dopamine is part of what helps our brain to naturally wake up.** So it's no wonder that when we get a lot of this right before we're trying to sleep that it becomes hard.

Trying to sleep while your phone is pinging and beeping with new notifications is impossible. In Step 6 we talked about how the Zeigarnik effect makes us want to have a conclusion to a conversation. Your brain starts wondering who it could be, what you might be missing out on, imagining all the fun you could be having. This sometimes feels like an impossible temptation to compete with when all you want to do is 'turn off' your brain and fall asleep... but **we can disarm this temptation!**

A GOOD NIGHT'S
SLEEP IS GOOD FOR
THE SOUL

# Five ways to limit screen time at bedtime

### TURN NOTIFICATION PINGS OFF

Put your phone on airplane mode an hour before bed. When you switch it back on in the morning, your notifications will come flooding through and you'll wake up with good feelings.

### USE NIGHT MODE

Blue-light filters on devices can reduce the impact blue light is having on your brain. However, it doesn't stop the feelings your brain gets from the activities that you are using your phone for, so it's only part of the solution.

### LISTEN, DON'T WATCH

Get any night-time entertainment in the form of podcasts rather than videos. There are even podcasts designed to relax you before bed.

### TAKE IT OUTSIDE

Charge your phone anywhere but in your bedroom. If it's not within arm's reach then the temptation to check it or use it when you're finding it hard to fall asleep won't be there.

### BRING IN BACKUP

If you're still finding using your phone at night super tempting, then ask your caregivers to hang on to your phone at night-time.

# Five ways to get a good night's sleep

## DO WHAT WORKS BEST FOR YOU

Different people need different amounts of sleep. Take time to understand how much sleep you need before you adjust anything else.

## GET OUTSIDE IN THE DAY

Make sure you get as much natural light as possible in the daytime, especially first thing in the morning. If you can add some exercise as well, that might help.

## BE CONSISTENT WITH TIMINGS

Try to sleep and wake up at the same time every day (even at the weekends). Avoid regular, long lie-ins as they can make it harder to fall asleep at night.

## START A ROUTINE

Build a calm bedtime routine such as putting on your pyjamas, brushing your teeth and reading a story. These activities can help to act as 'triggers' for your brain that it's time for bed.

## BE PATIENT WITH YOURSELF

Finally, if you can't get to sleep, try not to give yourself a hard time about it. Get up, do something relaxing for a few minutes, and then try again.

## Step 10

# Make Space for Joy

*JOY IS A FEELING OF GREAT PLEASURE OR HAPPINESS.*

*FOR US, THIS COMES FROM PURPOSE AND CONNECTION.*

When you're holding your phone in your hands, ask yourself, 'Does it help me fulfil my purpose? Does it help me create relationships and care for others? Does it help or hinder me from using my time and energy in other ways?'

# Joy is good for your body and mind.

When our phones become the most important thing in our lives it's easy to see how other important habits — getting outside in nature, exercising regularly, engaging with hobbies such as playing an instrument or reading a book — begin to drop off. This doesn't happen overnight, but gradually over time we may start to reduce these crucial parts of life. Each of these activities on their own can seem unimportant and even boring. This is why it can feel easy to stop them to gain a bit of extra time on our phones. But be warned! **When combined together, these activities are super important for keeping us happy and healthy.** This is a true reflection of how our phones can grab and keep our attention so well. You might have noticed this happen to someone else, or even felt that this was happening to you.

Let's take this chance to reflect on how many of the hobbies that bring you joy are on screens. This could include playing video games, posting on social media, editing videos or content creation, or watching TV or movies. Now think of how many of your hobbies don't involve screens. Which list was longer, and which was easier to think of? Do you have hobbies that you used to do? Why did you stop these? Maybe you just lost interest, maybe it became too hard to do, or maybe the pull of your phone dragged you away from them. Finally, do you have any hobbies or interests that you've wanted to try but have put off giving them a go? What has gotten in the way of these and how could you make it easier to try them?

**Children in our clinic often ask, 'Why is it so important that I have a variety of hobbies when I know exactly what I like to do?'** This is a great question. Remember in Step 4 we talked about the process of 'pruning' that you brain does as you grow up. **Well, when we only ever do similar activities (for example, using screens), then your brain learns that it doesn't need a lot of the information and abilities that you have learned as a kid and it gets rid of these.** Imagine your brain is made up of lots of interconnecting wires, almost like lots of overlapping spiderwebs. When you use lots of different parts of your brain (which is what you do when you have lots of different interests) you keep those valuable thread connections between different parts of your brain.

This helps you with creative thinking and problem solving.

Have you ever changed your mind about something? We certainly have. That's why it is so important to have a range of interests and hobbies. By telling your brain that these are important parts to keep, it makes sure that your brain is better equipped to do a variety of tasks. It's like sending your brain into combat wearing the latest legendary armour set and weapons versus equipping it with the starter gear.

*WE CAN CHOOSE JOY AND KEEP CHOOSING IT EVERY DAY.*

Perhaps you could choose to have screen and not-screen hobbies that support each other. Maybe you like skateboarding and video game design and want to create the next skateboarding video game, or maybe you love getting out in nature and photography. When we spend time doing other hobbies, we can even make use of our old friend 'state of flow'. By getting in the zone doing activities we love, we can become hyper-focused and surprise ourselves with our own abilities. You might even discover exciting new abilities that you never even realised you had.

**As you go on your journey to figure out how to have a healthy relationship with your phone, it is important to remember to take care of yourself no matter what.**

*FIND WHAT BRINGS YOU JOY SO THAT YOU CAN BE THE BEST POSSIBLE VERSION OF YOU THAT YOU CAN BE.*

If you're finding it hard to change your habits, don't get down on yourself. Sometimes we need to call in back-up. This is when making a precommitment can be a useful strategy. A precommitment is when you tell a friend or family member that you're going to commit to changing your behaviour. **When we tell another person about our intention to change our behaviour, we are much more likely to succeed.** And after all, they say the secret to happiness is helping others!

THE THINGS
THAT BRING US
TRUE JOY ARE
RARELY THINGS

# Five ways to make space for joy in your life

### TRY SOMETHING NEW

Trying new things increases your brain's ability to change and adapt. If you're anything like us, you've got a gazillion things on your 'someday' list... why wait? Try something new today.

### SPEND TIME IN NATURE

Spending as little as twenty minutes outside every day can be a game changer when it comes to feeling more joy in life, especially if nature experiences are a regular part of your routine.

### BUILD HEALTHY RELATIONSHIPS

Some of the greatest sources of joy can be the relationships we have with other people. One way to make space for joy in your life is to foster healthy and happy relationships.

### SET BOUNDARIES

Setting boundaries around screen time might sound scary, but it gives you the freedom to spend time doing what you love.

### MAKE A JOY LIST

Think of the ordinary, regular moments that just make you feel good, and write those down. Whatever your small and simple joy items are, know them and practise them!

## Five questions to ask to make space for joy in your life

Making time for yourself will do wonders for your wellbeing, health, relationships and schoolwork.
Ask yourself:

ARE YOU GIVING YOURSELF THE SPACE YOU NEED TO DO YOUR BEST WORK?

ARE YOU TAKING CARE OF YOUR BODY BY STRETCHING AND MOVING?

ARE YOU EATING AND DRINKING HEALTHILY?

ARE YOU SPENDING TIME WITH THOSE WHO MATTER MORE THAN YOUR PHONE EVER WILL?

ARE YOU GIVING YOURSELF TIME TO BREATHE AND BE PRESENT?

We know it can be hard to set aside time for joy, especially when you're battling against your phone. But let it creep into your life when you can. **Give joy space to be seen and experienced.**

# As we come to the end of the book, we wanted to share more about the relationship we have with our phones.

Throughout this book we have tried very hard to avoid coming across as 'two grumpy old men' telling young people how to use their phones. Partly because no one likes to be lectured. But mostly because we are coming from a place where we often get the balance wrong, too. **And there's nothing worse than someone telling you to 'do as I say, not as I do'.**

BRAD HAS DEDICATED THE LAST FIFTEEN YEARS OF HIS LIFE, BOTH IN THE CLINIC AND THE RESEARCH LAB, TO HEALTHY TECH AND SCREEN USE, BUT STILL STRUGGLES.

He recently went on a family holiday to Surfer's Paradise, Australia. It's an iconic Aussie destination with multiple theme parks. In the lead up to that holiday he was mindlessly checking his phone for what he thought was a minute but was more like ten, and became worried his phone would distract him from having fun with his family.

**He knew he had to find a way to take back control or risk it ruining his family holiday.** His solution? He left his phone at the hotel room for the day and bought a smartwatch. Sounds a bit strange to combat technology with more technology, we know! But on that smartwatch, he only had the basics: text messaging and phone calls. It worked a treat. He walked around Surfer's Paradise, explored the rides and had plenty of fun without any distraction. (On the one occasion his family was separated and he did look silly making a phone call on his watch like some kind of James Bond character, but that didn't matter. It was worth it!)

*AS FOR LINDSAY, CONCERNS OVER HIS TECHNOLOGY USAGE BEGAN IN HIGH SCHOOL.*

He was a little bit nerdy growing up. He loved all things tech-related — in particular, playing video games. This was his safe space: exploring new imaginary worlds with friends, meeting others who enjoyed games as much as he did, and pretending to be anyone and anything he wanted to be.

When World of Warcraft came along, he felt he had found everything he had been searching for. Before he knew it, he was hiding in his closet to skip school, just so he could stay home and play. He was barely sleeping, not completing schoolwork, and relying on energy drinks to get him through the day. He convinced himself this was normal. In fact, he thought he was a genius and had figured out a way to have it all — that he was in control.

Every year he told himself that he would quit and focus on his schooling and that he still had time to improve his grades. That never happened. He graduated high school with one of the lowest grades in his year. It made achieving his goals and dream job significantly harder.

That's when he realised that he had never been in control. **He was able to regain control by figuring out what genuinely motivated his desire to escape the 'real world' and then learning healthier ways to address those issues.**

Fast-forward to today, and he still plays video games with friends and uses technology throughout the day (a lot less than he used to, and he's glad about that!). Now it doesn't take away from the other areas of his life that are important to him. In fact, technology helps him pursue hobbies, do his job, and connect with people around the world. Technology helps build him up and enhance his experiences instead of replacing them.

*THE REALITY IS, TECHNOLOGY WILL ONLY INCREASE ITS FOOTPRINT IN YOUR LIFETIME.*

**We believe living sustainably with technology is the new frontier.** Acknowledging that we live in a world full of technology — which both creates opportunities and has the potential to steal our attention — allows us to take back control over how we live with it... and **armed with the information in the ten steps in this book we hope you can begin to thrive in this new frontier.**

EMBRACE THE
POWER OF THE
PRESENT
MOMENT AND
RELISH IN ITS
BEAUTY

ADDICTION — when your mind and body feels like it needs something in order to function.

AMYGDALA — a part of the brain that helps process and express emotions, especially fear.

APP — a piece of software that performs a function, like a game on a mobile phone.

AROUSAL — a state of being alert, or stimulated and active.

ARTIFICIAL INTELLIGENCE — a tool that allows computers or machines to 'think' or learn.

CIRCADIAN RHYTHM — human sleep-wake patterns (which include other functions such as body temperature) that operate on a twenty-four-hour cycle.

CLICKBAIT — online content designed to make audiences 'click' on eye-catching or sensational headlines or images for more information.

CLIMATE CHANGE — changes in the Earth's climate, especially the gradual rise in temperature caused by high levels of carbon dioxide.

CYBERBULLYING — an online form of bullying, where someone uses technology to threaten, shame or harass a person or group.

DETOX — reducing or removing something you believe is harmful or that you do too much of, such as eating sugar, from your daily life.

DIGITAL — a way of storing and showing information online rather than in print.

DOOMSCROLLING — consistently looking at negative stories or news through online devices or computers.

DOPAMINE — a chemical that the brain releases to make you feel good.

FREEZE RESPONSE — a physical response of 'shutting down' or 'freezing' when feeling overwhelmed or scared.

FUNCTIONALITY — how something functions, i.e. how many features a phone has.

GAMIFICATION — applying game-design strategies and elements to non-game features on a device, for example, the 'streaks' in Snapchat.

HABIT LOOP — a set of actions that makes a routine (something you do again and again, on a loop!).

HYPERPERSONAL EFFECT — strong emotions felt through online connections, which can sometimes be stronger than in-person meetings.

INDIVIDUATION — a time when young people or teens begin to separate themselves from a caregiver or parental influence, and become more their own person.

INTERMITTENT REINFORCEMENT—
when a reward or punishment is
given at irregular times and not to
any schedule.

LIMBIC SYSTEM — various parts
of the brain that deal with
emotions, especially 'fight-or-
flight response'.

MELATONIN — a chemical in the
brain that responds to darkness
and helps regulate your sleep-wake
cycle. See Circadian rhythm.

MINDFULNESS — being aware of
what you are doing and feeling in
the present moment.

MODELLING — a way of
learning by noticing and copying
others' behaviour.

NEAR-MISS EFFECT — the feeling
when you think you have nearly
won something, like a game.

NEGATIVE BIAS — when the
more negative or 'bad' things
seem to take on more importance,
or if you see something negatively
when it's not.

POP-UP — an image or ad that
suddenly 'pops up' on your screen.

PREFRONTAL CORTEX — the
decision-making part of the brain
still developing into the mid-20s
for humans.

PRIMITIVE — an early stage of
something, or something that
isn't yet developed.

PUSH NOTIFICATIONS — short
online messages sent by apps or
websites to your phone or
handheld device.

SELF-CARE — the practice of
looking after one's own wellbeing.

SHORT-FORM CONTENT — shorter-
length videos viewed online.

SNAP — a picture or video that is
deleted automatically once viewed,
used on Snapchat.

SOCIAL MEDIA — websites or apps
that allow users to interact or chat
with others online.

STATE OF FLOW — a feeling when
you are totally immersed in a task,
with time passing quickly.

STICKY — a website or app designed
to make the user stay on it for a
long time and 'stick' around.

STREAKS — a strategy used by
social media apps to keep you doing
something daily to keep up a
'streak': taking a daily picture or
finishing a puzzle, for example.

ZEIGARNIK EFFECT — the idea that
people are better at remembering
unfinished tasks than finished ones.

Find out more about how to better understand our relationships with our phones and other technologies and find ways to reconnect with the wider world with the help of an adult.

## BOOKS

**Dr Christian's Guide to Growing Up Online** by Dr Christian Jessen

**Social Media Survival Guide** by Holly Bathie

**Staying Safe Online** by Louie Stowell

**You're Crushing It!** by Lex Croucher

## PODCASTS

**The Healthy Screen Habits Podcast**
Insights and tips on healthy screen-time management for the whole family.

**Like You — Mindfulness for Kids**
Creates a calm, screen-free experience to learn and be empowered.

**Mostly Mindful for Teens and Tweens**
Quick mindfulness exercises to build resiliency.

## WEBSITES

**BBC: Own It**
Wellbeing advice and resources on ways to deal with phone usage.

www.bbc.com/ownit/take-control

**Centre for Humane Technology — Take Control and Youth Toolkit**
Tips on how to regain control of your phone use as well as a Youth Toolkit guide.

www.humanetech.com/take-control
www.humanetech.com/youth

**Turning Life On**
A site focused on digital wellness and communities.

www.turninglifeon.org/digital-wellness